Managing Editor
Ina Massler Levin, M.A.

Editor-in-Chief
Sharon Coan, M.S. Ed.

Illustrator
Sue Fullam

Cover Artist
Barb Lorseyedi

Art Director
CJae Froshay

Art Coordinator
Kevin Barnes

Product Manager
Phil Garcia

Publisher
Mary D. Smith, M.S. Ed.

Practice Makes Perfect

Reading Comprehension

GRADE 4

Author

Teacher Created Resources Staff

Teacher Created Resources, Inc.
6421 Industry Way
Westminster, CA 92683
www.teachercreated.com

ISBN: 978-0-7439-3334-6

©2002 Teacher Created Resources, Inc.
Reprinted, 2010
Made in U.S.A.

Table of Contents

Introduction

The old adage "practice makes perfect" can really hold true for your child and his or her education. The more practice and exposure your child has with concepts being taught in school, the more success he or she is likely to find. For many parents, knowing how to help their children may be frustrating because the resources may not be readily available.

As a parent it is also difficult to know where to focus your efforts so that the extra practice your child receives at home supports what he or she is learning in school.

This book has been written to help parents and teachers reinforce basic skills with children. *Practice Makes Perfect: Reading Comprehension* gives practice with reading and answering questions to help fully comprehend what is read. The exercises in this book can be done sequentially or can be taken out of order, as needed.

After reading the story the questions can be answered either by circling the answers or by reproducing and using the fill-in answer sheets found on pages 46 and 47. The practice tests, one for each of the areas of reading, can be bubbled in on the answer pages that are provided for each test.

The following standards or objectives will be met or reinforced by completing the practice pages included in this book. These standards and objectives are similar to the ones required by your state and school district. These standards and objectives are appropriate for the fourth grade.

- The student will demonstrate competence in making simple predictions about what is being read.
- The student will demonstrate competence in using various reading strategies to read the stories and answer the questions.
- The student will demonstrate competence in finding the main idea in a story, making inferences and making predictions.
- The student will be familiar with different types of reading (fiction, nonfiction, informational).
- The student will be able to use context clues and other aides to determine the meaning of a word.

How to Make the Most of This Book

Here are some useful ideas for making the most of this book:

- Set aside a specific place in your home to work on this book. Keep it neat and tidy with materials ready on hand.
- Set up a certain time of day to work on these practice pages to establish consistency, or look for times in your day or week that are less hectic and conducive to practicing skills.
- Keep all practice sessions with your child positive and constructive. If the mood becomes frustrated or tense, set the book aside and look for another time to practice with your child. Forcing your child to perform will not help. Do not use this book as a punishment.
- Help beginning readers with instructions.
- Review the work your child has done.
- Allow the child to use whatever writing instruments he or she prefers. For example, colored pencils can add variety and pleasure to drill work.
- Pay attention to the areas in which your child has the most difficulty. Provide extra guidance and exercises in those areas.
- Read aloud with your child and ask reading comprehension questions.

Fiction

Flea Market Find

Bethany loved to go with her mom and dad to the flea market. This Saturday morning was a perfect flea-market day, bright and sunny but not too warm. Mom turned the car onto the crunchy gravel road. A man in an old baseball cap stood in the road. Mom slowed down and gave the man a dollar. He handed her a ticket. Bethany smiled and waved at the man. He waved back.

Mom drove slowly, looking for a place to park. Bethany watched the people walking around the booths. Some booths had bright banners hanging from them. One read: Pillows For Sale, 2 For $20. Another said: All Shoes 50% OFF. A third said: The World's Biggest Waffles. Mom found a parking space and they all got out of the car.

They did the same thing every weekend. First, they went to Bubba's Hot Drinks stand. Mom and Dad bought coffee, and Bethany got hot chocolate. Mom and Bethany shared a blueberry muffin while Dad ate a bagel. After they ate, it was time to shop!

There was always something new at the flea market. Bethany, Mom, and Dad wandered from booth to booth. Mom bought a bunch of dried flowers. Dad looked at all the shiny tools in the tool booth. One man had a booth filled with wind-up toys. Bethany laughed at the wind-up toy dog that barked and jumped.

"Do you see anything you like?" Mom asked. Bethany looked around. One booth had hundreds of sweet-smelling candles. In another booth, an artist had paintings for sale. A gray-haired woman in a purple hat sold old curtains. A man wearing a turban had a booth filled with rugs.

"Not yet, Mom," Bethany said. "I'll keep looking, though."

Sometimes Mom stopped to look at something. Dad wandered off to a booth filled with old boat parts. Bethany tasted a sample of homemade fudge that one vendor was giving away. As she chewed the crumbly fudge, her eye caught a booth she had never seen before. It was filled with old stuff. A pile of crates stood in one corner. Wooden picture frames leaned against each other beside a pile of bed frames. Sitting on top of a pile of quilts was an old rag doll.

Bethany looked closely at the doll. The doll had seen better days. Her brown yarn hair was twisted and matted. Bethany could see that her dress had been pretty once, but now it was dirty and torn. The doll was made out of purple fabric with tiny pink flowers, and one of her shoes was missing. As tattered as it was, there was something about the doll that Bethany liked.

Bethany's mom and dad came up behind her. "She looks pretty torn up, honey," Mom said. "Are you sure you want her?"

Bethany studied the doll's face. The doll's black-bead eyes looked calmly back.

"Yes, she needs a good home," Bethany said. "Can I have her?"

"Sure," Mom said. After they paid the man at the booth, Bethany carried the doll carefully back to the car. Bethany held her new doll. Yes, there was no doubt about it; she loved the flea market!

Flea Market Find (cont.)

Reading Comprehension Questions

After reading the story answer the questions. Circle the correct answer.

1. Mom drove slowly in order to—
   a. buy some waffles
   b. find a place to park
   c. look at the shiny tools
   d. pay for the rag doll

2. One of the banners read—
   a. Pillows, 50% OFF
   b. All Shoes, 50% OFF
   c. World's Biggest Pillows
   d. Bagels, 2 For $1

3. The story could also be called—
   a. "Mom's Day at the Flea Market"
   b. "Bethany's Special Doll"
   c. "Dad Likes Tools"
   d. "Saturday Shopping Spree"

4. How did Bethany probably feel at the end of the story?
   a. Angry
   b. Happy
   c. Upset
   d. Sad

5. According to the story, Bethany is the kind of girl who—
   a. likes to sit on top of a pile of quilts
   b. eats a lot of waffles
   c. enjoys seeing and finding all sorts of things
   d. does not like to go to the flea market with her parents

Mona Wants A Dog

Ever since her friend Claire got a dog last year, Mona had wanted a dog. Mona got to play with Claire's dog every time she went over to Claire's house, which made her want one even more. Mona couldn't stop thinking about it. She checked out books from the library about dogs. She learned what to feed them and when to feed them. She knew the right kinds of toys to give puppies. She knew what kinds of toys older dogs like.

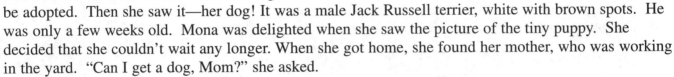

Whenever she had time after school, Mona would go to the computer lab. She liked to look at her favorite Web site, "Dog Lover's Heaven." It had lists of dogs that were available in her area. She could also find out about every kind of dog in the world. Sometimes, Mona would read about dogs just because their names sounded interesting, like Lhasa apso or Pug. But Mona knew she wanted a Jack Russell terrier because Jack Russells are small and very smart dogs.

One day after school, Mona visited the "Dog Lover's Heaven" Web site to see what dogs could be adopted. Then she saw it—her dog! It was a male Jack Russell terrier, white with brown spots. He was only a few weeks old. Mona was delighted when she saw the picture of the tiny puppy. She decided that she couldn't wait any longer. When she got home, she found her mother, who was working in the yard. "Can I get a dog, Mom?" she asked.

"We've talked about this, Mona," Mom said. "We have to be sure you can take care of it. It's a lot of work to own a dog."

"But I've done lots of research, Mom," Mona explained.

"I know, but I need to be sure. A dog has to be fed and have lots of water. You have to take it for walks so it can get exercise. Are you ready to do that every day after school, even if you're tired or it's raining?" Mom asked.

"Yes, Mom. I know it's important to you that I take care of it all by myself," Mona said.

"If you get a puppy, it may not be housebroken. Are you going to clean up after it?" Mom asked.

Mona thought for a moment. She knew she wasn't going to like every single thing about owning a dog. Still, a little extra work was a small price to pay for having a great dog. "Yes, Mom," she said. "I will."

"All right, I believe you. Remember what I said about saving your money to pay for the things the dog will need?"

"Yes, Mom," Mona said. "I saved enough already for the Humane Society's adoption fee and for the first visit to the vet. I have been thinking about this for a long time."

"Great!" Mom said. "Then we'll go this weekend. Do you know what kind of dog you want?"

"I sure do," Mona said with a smile. "And I can't wait to meet him!"

Mona Wants a Dog *(cont.)*

1. Mona wanted a dog because—
    a. her friend Claire got a dog last year
    b. she saw a cute commercial on TV
    c. she walks by a pet store every day
    d. her teacher talks about her dog

2. What type of dog does Mona want?
    a. Boston terrier
    b. Lhasa apso
    c. Pug
    d. Jack Russell terrier

3. What does Mona mean when she says "a little extra work was a small price to pay for having a great dog"?
    a. Mona will get a job to help pay for the puppy.
    b. Mona's mom will have to work more hours to afford a puppy.
    c. The dog was on sale, and Mona could work at the pet store.
    d. Mona will not mind cleaning up after a dog.

4. What does Mona's mother mean when she says, "It's a lot of work to own a dog"?
    a. Mona needs to do more research before she is ready to own a dog.
    b. Dogs work hard to be good pets for people.
    c. Dogs have to be fed and exercised every day and cleaned up after.
    d. Mona will need more rest if she gets a dog.

5. How did Mona learn so much about dogs?
    a. Listening to her teacher at school
    b. Visiting an Internet Web site
    c. Writing to the Humane Society
    d. Watching a videotape about dogs

My Cousin Douglas

I first met my cousin Douglas when he came to stay with my family for a year. His parents were going to teach in Africa, but they thought it might be better for him to stay in this country to go to school.

It was strange to see him. He and his family lived all the way on the other side of the country, so we had never had a chance to visit. He was just someone I sent birthday cards to and saw in snapshots. Now he was going to stay and go to school with me.

We met him at the airport. It was not hard to figure out which person was Douglas, even if we had never seen pictures of him. He was the one standing all alone, looking around for someone to meet him. Everyone in my family has light brown hair and green eyes, but Douglas has dark hair and dark eyes. He looked a little scared to meet us. He started to smile shyly after Mother hugged him.

Before Douglas arrived, Mother had spoken to me about making sure he felt welcome. "I don't want you playing any of your tricks on him," she warned me.

I had not planned to play any tricks on him. I was happy at the thought of having someone like a brother. I just have two sisters, and, except for playing tricks, I do not have much fun with them.

When we got back home and Douglas started putting his things away, I could not believe it. All of his clothes were the same, all white shirts and dark blue shorts. He even had a dark blue jacket with a tie!

"How come you wear only one kind of clothes?" I asked him.

"That's the way my school has always been," he said. "It's a private school, and we have to wear uniforms."

"Yuck," I said. "I would hate having to wear the same thing every day."

Douglas shrugged. "I don't mind," he said. "It saves time. I don't have to think about what I am going to wear."

"Well, we don't wear uniforms at our school. You're going to look pretty funny if you come to school in a jacket and tie."

Douglas looked worried. Suddenly, I felt bad. I had not meant to hurt his feelings. After all, it was not easy to come all this way to live with some strange family for a year. Then and there I decided that I was going to look after my cousin and try to make this as good a year as possible for him.

My Cousin Douglas (cont.)

1. This story teaches the author a lesson. What lesson does he learn?

    a. You should wear uniforms.

    b. You should look after family.

    c. You should make fun of people.

    d. You should play tricks on people.

2. Which quotation from the passage helped you to answer the previous question?

    a. "Then and there I decided that I was going to look after my cousin."

    b. "I have just two sisters and do not have much fun with them."

    c. "I was happy at the thought of having someone like a brother."

    d. "He was the one standing all alone, looking around for someone to meet him."

3. Douglas is coming to live with the author's family because—

    a. his parents wanted him to stay in school in his own country

    b. the author needed someone besides his sisters to play with

    c. he wanted to get to know his cousins better

    d. his parents wanted him to attend private school

4. At the end of the story, the author suddenly felt bad because he—

    a. did not have nice clothes like Douglas had

    b. had hurt Douglas's feelings

    c. did not want Douglas to live with them

    d. had played too many tricks on his sisters

5. Why were Douglas's clothes all the same?

    a. He liked only blue shorts and white shirts.

    b. Those were the only clothes sold in Africa.

    c. His old school required him to wear a uniform.

    d. He had trouble deciding what to wear.

The Chess Champion

Pedro looked down at the chessboard and swallowed. He always got nervous just before a match, and today was no exception. Today was the big chess tournament. All the schools had sent their best players to compete at the convention center downtown. Yet, here sat Pedro, waiting to make his first move.

Pedro was not exactly the best chess player in his school. Rashid was better than he was. Rashid had won the match to decide which student from Carver Middle School would qualify for the tournament. Rashid had come down with the flu, though, so now Pedro was here to take his place.

The girl across the board from Pedro looked really tough. Her name was Jasmine, and she had come in third in the state last year. The more Pedro looked at her intent face, the less likely he thought that he could beat her. He looked down at the board again.

In front of him were 16 white chess pieces. The pawns were the weakest and least important pieces. There were eight of them, facing the pieces across the board. Behind the pawns were the king, the queen, two bishops, two knights, and two rooks. Somehow Pedro had to protect his king while capturing Jasmine's king. It was not going to be easy.

Pedro nervously moved one of his pawns. The game had started. Jasmine quickly moved one of her pawns. Pedro moved another pawn. Jasmine did the same. So far, it was not so bad. In fact, Jasmine was using the same moves that most of Pedro's usual opponents used.

After 15 minutes, Pedro realized that Jasmine was not quite so tough after all. She was starting to make little mistakes. Once, she almost made a move that would have left her king open. She seemed to be in a hurry, trying to get Pedro to move his pieces quickly. Pedro refused to let her rush him. He took his time.

Then, all at once, he saw his chance. If he moved his queen in front of Jasmine's rook, he would be able to win. He moved his queen, leaving his finger on top of it. As long as he was touching his playing piece, his move was not yet over. He pretended to hesitate; then he took his finger off.

Bam! Jasmine took his queen with her rook, almost knocking it off the table. "Ha!" she laughed. "Take that!"

Pedro smiled. "I'll take your king," he said. "Checkmate."

The Chess Champion (cont.)

1. Jasmine said, "Ha! Take that!" because she—
    a. wanted Pedro to take her rook
    b. wanted to scare Pedro
    c. thought Pedro's joke was funny
    d. thought Pedro had made a mistake

2. Pedro made sure he played slowly because—
    a. he might make mistakes if he rushed
    b. Rashid had told him to play that way
    c. he wanted Jasmine to get bored and quit
    d. tournament rules said to play slowly

3. How does Pedro feel at the end of the story?
    a. Sorry that Jasmine lost
    b. Sad because he lost his queen
    c. Disappointed that he had made mistakes
    d. Happy because he won

4. Why did Pedro stare at the board before the game even started?
    a. If he looked around the convention center, he would lose his focus.
    b. If he looked at Jasmine, his doubts about winning increased.
    c. He needed to decide what move he wanted to make first.
    d. The tournament officials wanted him to count his chess pieces.

5. Which sentence from the passage helps you answer the previous question?
    a. In fact, Jasmine was using the same moves that most of Pedro's usual opponents used.
    b. The more Pedro looked at her intent face, the less likely he thought that he could beat her.
    c. If he moved his queen in front of Jasmine's rook, he would be able to win.
    d. As long he was touching his playing piece, his move was not yet over.

Starting a Business

Stephanie and Becky had lived next door to each other for as long as they could remember. When they turned seven, both girls received puppies for their birthdays. They worked very hard training the puppies. When the girls were nine, they had two very well trained dogs.

"I think that we did a good job training our dogs," Becky said one day. "What do you think about the idea of starting a dog training business?"

Stephanie's ears perked up. "I think that's a great idea!' she exclaimed. "Let's get started right away."

The girls began their new business by making some flyers on Becky's computer. Then, they hopped on their bikes and pedaled through the neighborhood, passing out the flyers. Many of Stephanie and Becky's neighbors had seen the girls training their own dogs, and were very impressed. It wasn't long before the phone was ringing off the hook and the girls had a lot of customers.

During the next few weeks, Becky and Stephanie trained almost every dog in the neighborhood. They worked just as hard as they had with their own dogs. Soon the neighborhood dogs were sitting, fetching, and walking on leashes. The girls received a lot of praise from their customers and were thrilled with their own success.

"Let's send notes thanking everyone for their business," suggested Stephanie. "That way we're sure to get more customers next summer!"

"Now that's what I call a great idea!" Becky laughed.

Starting a Business *(cont.)*

1. How does the author present Stephanie and Becky?

    a. As computer experts

    b. As excited and hard-working

    c. As people with a lot of pets

    d. As difficult to get along with

2. How did the girls' customers probably feel after Stephanie and Becky trained the customer's dogs?

    a. Angry

    b. Disappointed

    c. Upset

    d. Glad

3. Which word best describes Stephanie and Becky as they started their new business?

    a. Eager

    b. Careful

    c. Lazy

    d. Hasty

4. What is the main idea of this passage?

    a. Stephanie and Becky both received dogs for their seventh birthday.

    b. The neighbors noticed that Stephanie and Becky did a great job training their own dogs.

    c. Stephanie and Becky sent out flyers to advertise their business.

    d. Stephanie and Becky started successful a dog training business.

5. What does "ringing off the hook" mean?

    a. The phone was ringing all the time.

    b. The phone fell off a hook that it was hanging on.

    c. The ringing of the phone sounded like a hook.

    d. A hook made the phone ring.

New Faces

When Laticia was nine years old, her family decided to move across the country to California. Her mother had found a good job in California, and her father's company was willing to transfer him so he, too, could work in California. Before they moved, her parents had to take a trip to California to find a house where they would live.

"We will be gone for two weeks," Mother said. "While we are gone, you will stay with Aunt Betsy."

Aunt Betsy lived several hours away, in a big city. Laticia had never stayed with Aunt Betsy, so she didn't know what to pack for her visit. The weather was warm, so she put some shorts and T-shirts in a suitcase. Then she thought that maybe nobody wore shorts in the city, so she packed a dress and a pair of pants, too. She put books in another bag. Laticia liked reading. Mostly she was reading books about horses. Probably nobody would read books about horses in the city. Horses were country animals.

When the day came, Aunt Betsy drove to Laticia's house to pick her up. After they all had lunch, Laticia and Aunt Betsy dropped Laticia's mother and father off at the airport.

"Have a good visit," Mother said.

"You take care of yourself," Father said.

Laticia hugged them both good-bye.

Aunt Betsy's car was big and new. They kept the windows rolled up and the air-conditioning on as they drove to the city. Laticia watched the country pass by outside the car windows. Sometimes she saw horses in the fields. Laticia wished she could have a horse some day.

When they got to Aunt Betsy's, Laticia saw it was a high-rise apartment complex instead of a house. Aunt Betsy carried Laticia's suitcase for her. Laticia carried her own bag of books. Inside, Aunt Betsy said, "Here's your room," and she turned on a light switch. It was a small bedroom with a white bedspread on the bed. It was a nice room, but a little empty.

Then Laticia noticed something on the nightstand. She leaned close and saw it was a picture of a tall, reddish-brown horse! The horse had a black mane and a black tail. Aunt Betsy was in the picture, standing beside the horse.

"That's Ruby," Aunt Betsy said.

Laticia asked, "Is that your horse?"

Aunt Betsy said, "No, I ride her sometimes. She belongs to a stable not far away."

Laticia emptied her book bag onto the bed. She said, "I love horses. Everything I read is about horses." She asked, "Can we go visit Ruby?"

Aunt Betsy smiled. She said, "Of course. I'd love to visit Ruby. We can even go out riding."

Laticia felt better. She and her aunt had something in common. It was going to be a vacation and an adventure!

New Faces (cont.)

1. Aunt Betsy lived in a high-rise complex instead of a house. A complex is a large—
   a. office
   b. trailer
   c. building
   d. farm

2. What do Laticia and her aunt have in common?
   a. They both live in an apartment.
   b. They both love horses.
   c. They have the same last name.
   d. They are both moving to California.

3. What would be the best way to find the answer to the previous question?
   a. Look for people's names.
   b. List the places where the action happens.
   c. Find the important statements in the story.
   d. Skim the story again.

4. This story is mostly about—
   a. learning how to ride a horse
   b. a girl's visit to her aunt's home
   c. life in the big city
   d. moving across country

5. How does Laticia feel at the end of the story?
   a. Sad because she misses her mom and dad
   b. Excited because she will get to go horseback riding
   c. Happy because she is eager to move to California
   d. Upset because she will have to leave all of her friends

Ladybugs

Have you ever seen a small red beetle with black dots on its back? These little creatures are called lady beetles or ladybugs. Ladybugs are harmless insects. They do not bite or sting humans. They do not harm plants or carry diseases, either. In fact, ladybugs are quite helpful. Farmers and gardeners both like to see them on their plants. Why is that? It is because of what ladybugs eat.

Aphids are tiny insects that are harmful to many plants. Aphids suck the juices from plant leaves. This causes the leaves to shrivel up and die. Ladybugs have large appetites, and their favorite food is aphids. A ladybug can eat as many as 50 of them in a single day. For this reason, some people actually buy ladybugs at their garden store and set them free in their gardens.

Another advantage to having ladybugs in your garden is that you do not have to use insect poison to kill aphids. Many people, especially those growing fruits and vegetables, do not want to use poison on their plants. Letting ladybugs keep the number of aphids down is a natural way to grow healthy plants.

So if you happen to see a ladybug in a park or a garden, make sure to remember how helpful it can be. It might save your favorite plant one day!

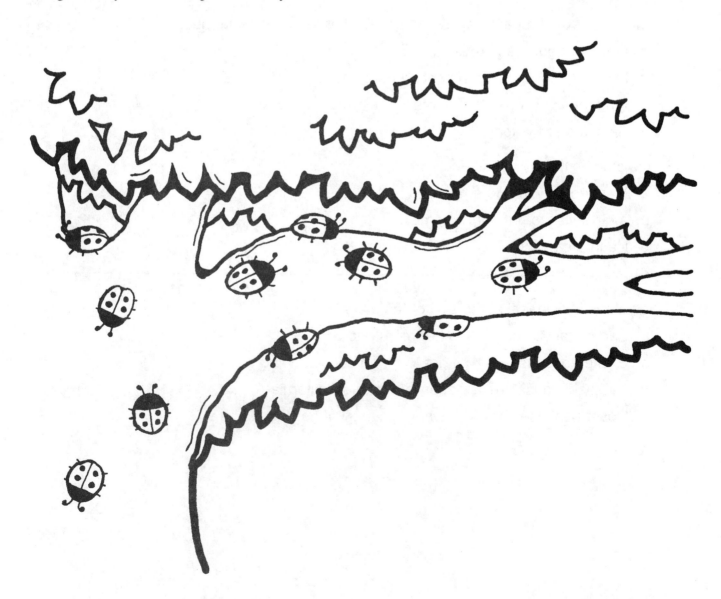

Ladybugs *(cont.)*

1. This passage is mostly about—

    a. how ladybugs do not bite humans

    b. how many aphids a ladybug can eat

    c. how to recognize a ladybug

    d. how ladybugs help farmers and gardeners

2. The author says that ladybugs are harmless to humans. Which sentence supports that statement?

    a. Ladybugs have large appetites.

    b. Ladybugs are red with black spots.

    c. Ladybugs do not bite or sting.

    d. Ladybugs are found all across the U.S.

3. Why would some people not want to put insect poison on fruit and vegetable plants?

    a. They do not want to kill aphids.

    b. They do not want poison on their food.

    c. They do not know where to buy poison.

    d. They worry that the plants will die.

4. How does the passage compare aphids to ladybugs?

    a. Aphids are more destructive to a garden than ladybugs.

    b. Aphids are prettier than ladybugs.

    c. Aphids are more colorful than ladybugs.

    d. Aphids are hungrier than ladybugs.

5. According to the story another name for a ladybug is

    a. lady flyer.

    b. aphid eater.

    c. lady bird.

    d. lady beetle.

Egyptian Pyramids

The pyramids of Egypt are well known throughout the world. Many people go to Egypt just to see these structures. There are more than 80 pyramids in Egypt today.

The pyramids were built as tombs, or burial rooms, for ancient Egyptian pharaohs (kings). The Egyptians wrapped the pharaohs' bodies with cloth before they were buried. They called this process mummification. The pharaohs were often buried with gold and treasures. These treasures usually filled several rooms inside the pyramid, with the king's body being buried in the innermost room.

It was thought for a long time that slaves built all the pyramids in Egypt. It was later found that farmers built most of the pyramids during the rainy season. When the Nile River flooded their fields, the farmers would work on the pyramids to make extra money.

The oldest pyramid in Egypt is the Step Pyramid. It was built in 2650 B.C. Like many other pyramids, the Step Pyramid was built with a maze of underground passages beneath it. The ancient builders hoped that the passages would prevent grave robbers from finding the rooms with the pharaohs' treasures. Despite these efforts, grave robbers did manage to steal many of the mummies and treasures from the pyramids. Scientists have found very few tombs with their mummies and their treasures untouched.

The biggest pyramid is the Great Pyramid. It stands 481 feet tall. It was the tallest structure on Earth until 1889, when the Eiffel Tower was built in France. The Great Pyramid is over 4,500 years old and is made up of several million blocks of stone. Each stone block weighs about 15 tons, or about the weight of eight school buses. The ancient Egyptians did not have cranes or tractors, and to this day, scientists don't know how they moved stones of this size and weight. They also didn't have cement or mortar. The Egyptians were able to measure the blocks so perfectly that they could stack one on top of another very tightly. The blocks are assembled so closely, in fact, that a piece of paper cannot be placed between them.

Egypt has a very dry climate. That means that art, pottery, or any other items that were buried with the mummies did not decay very quickly. Although these tombs are thousands of years old, they contain nearly perfect examples of life during an ancient era. Scientists have been able to learn an enormous amount about the way the ancient Egyptians lived by examining these amazing structures and the treasures they were built to hold.

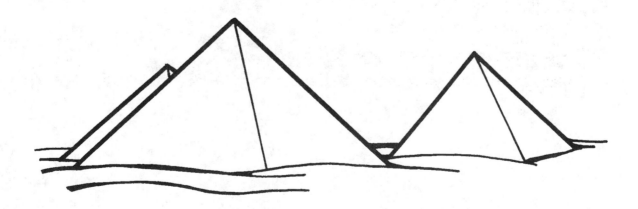

Egyptian Pyramids *(cont.)*

1. The pyramids were built as—

    a. palaces

    b. towers

    c. schools

    d. tombs

2. What is the height of the Great Pyramid?

    a. 1,889 feet

    b. 15 feet

    c. 4,500 feet

    d. 481 feet

3. Scientists want to study the pyramids because they want to—

    a. learn about life in ancient Egypt

    b. make Egyptian pottery

    c. build a pyramid

    d. get rich from the treasures

4. Why did the author include the fifth paragraph?

    a. To tell why the pyramids were built

    b. To introduce the idea that scientists don't know how the pyramids were built

    c. To discuss the climate of Egypt

    d. To discuss how grave robbers were able to enter the pyramids

5. What happened right before a pharaoh was buried?

    a. A pharaoh's riches were divided among his farmers.

    b. His treasures were removed from his pyramid.

    c. The pharaoh's body was wrapped with cloth.

    d. A place for the body was prepared near the door.

Hot Dogs

A snack seen at baseball games, racetracks, or your backyard barbecue, hot dogs are one of the most popular foods in America. Every hour 1.88 million hot dogs are produced in the United States. On average, every person in the United States eats about 1.2 hot dogs every week. There aren't many foods that were invented in America, but the hot dog is one of them. It's very similar to the sausage that comes from Germany. When did the sausage come to America? How did the sausage become the hot dog? Where did the name "hot dog" come from?

In the 1880s, a man named Charles Feltman moved to America from Frankfurt, Germany. Shortly after he came to America, Feltman sold cold pies from a food cart in Coney Island, New York. But Feltman had competition. He wasn't selling many pies because people preferred to eat in the hotels and restaurants, where they could sit down to eat heated food. Feltman's friends suggested that he sell hot foods, because people might like something warm to eat even if they were too busy to sit down.

Feltman decided to sell something people ate in his old hometown called the frankfurter. He made one important change, though. People in Germany usually ate frankfurters from a plate with a fork. Feltman put the sausage on a bun, covered it with mustard, and offered sauerkraut with it. He called it the "frankfurter sandwich." People loved Feltman's new creation, and the frankfurter sandwich became very popular. Feltman's business grew quickly. Soon, he was able to open his own restaurant.

When did people start calling the frankfurter sandwich a hot dog? At first Feltman's invention was known by many names. People called the frankfurter sandwiches "franks," "red-hots," or "wieners." One day in 1916, a cartoonist named Tad Dorgan was at a baseball game. He heard the frankfurter sellers yelling, "Get your red-hot dachshund sausages!" This gave Dorgan an idea for a new cartoon. Dachshunds are long skinny dogs with short legs. They are shaped very much like a sausage. Dorgan drew a cartoon of a dachshund inside a bun, as if it were a sausage with mustard on it. Dorgan didn't know how to spell the name of the dog, so when he drew the sausage seller, he made him yell, "Get your hot dogs!" The name stuck, and now most people know Charles Feltman's frankfurter sandwich as the "hot dog."

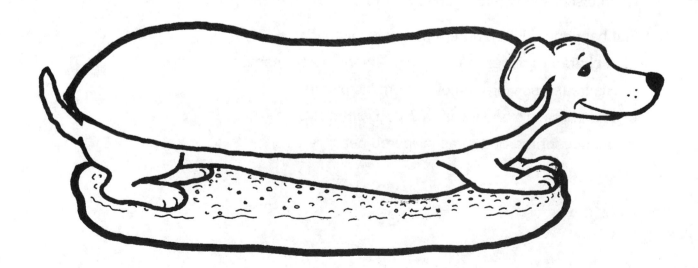

Hot Dogs *(cont.)*

1. Why was Charles Feltman having trouble selling his cold pies?

    a. People preferred to eat heated food in hotels and restaurants.

    b. Feltman was from Frankfurt, Germany.

    c. The cold pies did not taste very good.

    d. People preferred hot dogs.

2. What did Charles Feltman call his creation of a sausage on a bun with mustard?

    a. Hot dog

    b. Cold pie

    c. Hot dachshund

    d. Frankfurter sandwich

3. Ted Dorgan wrote "Get your hot dogs!" at the bottom of his cartoon because he—

    a. did not want people to call the treat "franks," "red-hots," or "wieners" anymore

    b. wanted to be the first person to invent a name for the treat

    c. did not know how to spell "dachshund"

    d. wanted to sell hot dogs at baseball games

4. How did Feltman probably feel when his creation became popular?

    a. Glad

    b. Tired

    c. Disappointed

    d. Puzzled

5. You can tell from the passage that the hot dog—

    a. is not very popular

    b. has an interesting history

    c. was named in Germany

    d. is usually served with mustard

Galaxies

Have you ever looked up in the night sky when you were far away from any city lights? Did you see a faintly shining band of light across the sky? This band of light is called the Milky Way, which is home to our planet Earth. It is made up of billions of stars, like our sun. These stars are too faint and far away to been seen individually. But because there are so many, we see them as a milky, white glow in the sky. All these stars are part of our galaxy—our neighborhood in the universe.

A galaxy is held together by a force called gravity. Gravity is a force that pulls objects together. When many objects that are nearly the same size come close together in space, they tend to stay held together by this force. Galaxies are like islands of stars in the huge ocean of outer space.

Galaxies are named by their shape. For example, a spiral galaxy, such as the Milky Way, is shaped like a flat disk with a bump in the center. From the top, the disk looks like a pinwheel. It has bright spiral arms that curl out from the center. Other galaxies are much rounder and do not have arms like spiral galaxies. Some galaxies may have run into others in the past and now have no clear shape at all.

When you think about galaxies, you might be amazed by the size of the universe. Our planet is just one of many that orbits the sun. The sun itself is just one star among billions of stars in our galaxy. Our galaxy is only one of billions of galaxies in the universe. So the next time you are away from the city lights at night, look up at the lights of our galaxy. It's a reminder of the amazing universe we live in.

Galaxies *(cont.)*

1. This passage is mostly about—
    a. gravity
    b. what galaxies are made of
    c. the night sky
    d. the sun

2. To look at the galaxy you would want to be away from the city because—
    a. there are many neighborhoods in the city
    b. there are no galaxies in the city sky
    c. the city lights make it difficult to see the galaxy
    d. the city is too noisy

3. The author compares galaxies to—
    a. a force of gravity
    b. the size of the universe
    c. glowing city lights
    d. islands of stars

4. What does the planet Earth orbit?
    a. The Milky Way
    b. A pinwheel
    c. The sun
    d. The universe

5. There are
    a. millions of stars in our galaxy.
    b. trillions of stars in our galaxy.
    c. billions of stars in our galaxy.
    d. thousands of stars in our galaxy.

How Do You "Howdy Do"?

When two people meet, their greetings to each other often involve more than the words they say. Not only are there a lot of ways to say hello, there are a lot of ways to show hello. The hand motions or other body movements that people make when they meet are as important as saying the right words. However, these body movements are not the same for everybody.

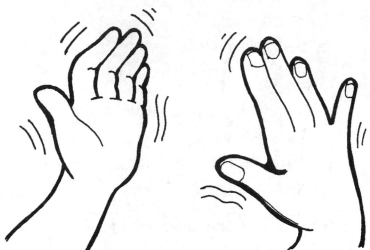

In America, people usually greet each other with a handshake to show respect for the other person. Athletes from opposite teams shake hands before a game to show respect for each other. Business people shake hands for the same reason. However, most Americans don't shake hands when they meet people they already know well. When American friends meet each other, they might only wave, slap palms, or maybe just nod their heads. They could say "hello" without making any special motions at all.

Military people use a special greeting called a salute. When two people of different ranks greet for the first time each day, they raise their right hands to touch their own foreheads. This custom may have come from the days when knights wore helmets with visors that covered their eyes. A knight had to lift the visor off of his eyes so people could see who he was.

In New Zealand, people touch their foreheads when they meet. This is an old tradition that comes from the Maori, who were the first people to live in New Zealand. Even today, people of all backgrounds in New Zealand touch their foreheads when they meet.

Kissing is sometimes used as a way to greet someone. In some countries, important people used to wear special rings. It was the custom for visitors to kiss these rings when they came for a meeting. In France, when people meet, they still sometimes kiss each other on the cheek as a sign of affection or respect.

Traditional Japanese culture is very formal. People bow to each other every time they meet. Even family members bow to each other. People decide how low to bow based on how respected the other person is. When two people who have the same status or job meet, they each bow as low as the other person.

Today, new ways of greeting are created all the time. People can say or show hello any way they choose. They can do this with a quick "hi," a handshake, or even a simple smile. The important thing is that the people they are greeting understand them.

How Do You "Howdy Do"? *(cont.)*

1. According to the passage, how do people of different ranks in the military greet each other for the first time each day?

   a. By saluting

   b. By kissing

   c. By shaking hands

   d. By touching foreheads

2. Another good name for this passage is—

   a. "Greetings!"

   b. "New Zealand and Japan"

   c. "Old Traditions"

   d. "Formal and Informal Cultures"

3. You can tell that people all over the world—

   a. do not like each other very much

   b. shake hands when they meet

   c. think of new ideas

   d. greet each other in different ways

4. The writer probably wrote this passage to—

   a. show that people greet each other in different ways

   b. explain that shaking hands is usually only done the first time you meet someone

   c. discuss kissing rings in France

   d. compare the military with other people

5. If you wanted to find out more about this, you could—

   a. read a book about Japanese culture

   b. watch a television program about greeting customs around the world

   c. meet somebody from New Zealand

   d. watch a television program about knights and their armor

Lighting the Way

Today, almost every home in America has electric lights. In the 1870s, things were very different. Back then, homes were lit by lamps that used gas or oil. The flames were dangerous and fires were common.

At this time, Joseph Swan was an inventor in England and Thomas Edison was an American inventor. The two men were racing each other to bring light, in the form of electricity, into people's homes. Each wanted to be the first to create a working light bulb.

The problem both inventors faced was how to make a bulb glow. In a light bulb, electricity flows through a thin strip of material called a filament. The filament glows white-hot and creates light. Edison and Swan experimented with many different types of filaments. They tried almost every material they could think of—from iron to paper. They even tried different kinds of hair! Each material they tested either did not light at all or caught on fire and burned out after only a few seconds.

Then, at almost the same time, Swan and Edison had success using carbon for the filament. This worked very well, and the bulb stayed lit for several hours. Swan registered his patent for the light bulb in 1878. Edison received his patent about a year later. The first light bulbs lasted only about 150 hours. Within four years, Edison made a bulb that lasted 1,200 hours. Today, light bulbs glow for about 2,000 hours.

Thomas Edison may not have been the first person to patent the light bulb, but he was the first person to bring electricity into people's homes. Edison designed the first electric power plant, called the Pearl Street Power Station in New York City. In 1882, it provided 203 people with power, but that number increased very quickly. By 1900, ten thousand people had electricity in their homes. By 1910 the number was already up to ten million.

At first Joseph Swan and Thomas Edison accused each other of stealing ideas. Eventually, they agreed to work together and co-founded an electric power company. Today this company is called Consolidated Edison.

Thomas Edison   **Joseph Swan**

Lighting the Way *(cont.)*

1. What is this passage mainly about?

    a. Joseph Swan's invention of the light bulb

    b. Thomas Edison's invention of the light bulb

    c. The history of the light bulb

    d. The start of a power company

2. In the last paragraph, what does the word "accuse" mean?

    a. To blame someone for something

    b. To copy someone's idea

    c. To be jealous of another person

    d. To work on the same project

3. How does the author develop the third paragraph?

    a. He tells how long the first light bulbs lasted.

    b. He suggests how the inventors could have worked together.

    c. He tells how dangerous early gas lit lamps were.

    d. He lists the difficulties of finding a good filament.

4. In the second paragraph, what does the phrase "bring electricity into people's homes" mean?

    a. Edison visited many people's homes.

    b. Electricity can be carried by a person.

    c. Edison's ideas helped people to get electricity.

    d. People like living in homes with electricity.

5. The description of the two inventors as "racing" each other to invent the light bulb suggests that they—

    a. were each trying to be the first to invent the light bulb.

    b. were working to start an electric company.

    c. did not personally like each other.

    d. only had a limited amount of time to invent the light bulb.

Community Message Board

Choir Practice

7:30 every Wednesday night. 10th Street Baptist Church. Meet in fellowship hall.

Karate Classes

Teacher has a black belt in karate. Two classes weekly, Wed. and Thurs., 6 p.m. Learn to defend yourself and have fun!

Volunteer Firehouse Pancake Supper, Saturday 5 p.m.–7 p.m.

Moving Sale

56 East Grove Street

Selling furniture, toys, clothes, a bike. Washer and dryer, $100.00 for both

Need your lawn mowed?

I will work hard. Call Mike at: 555-8721

Little League Tryouts

Little League tryouts this Saturday afternoon at 1:00. Call Brad at 555-2941 for more information. Bring your own glove.

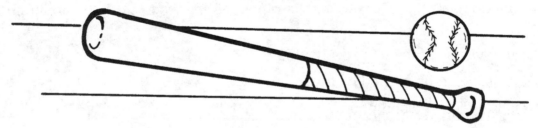

Dog Wash in Marlow Park.

Bring your dog. We'll wash it! $5.00 per dog. Flea dip extra. Call Lisa at 555-0971 for more information.

New Day to Recycle is Wednesday

Recycling pick-up day has been changed. It is now Wednesday. Be sure to put your recycling on the curb before 8:00 a.m.

Community Message Board (cont.)

1. When should you put your recycling on the curb?

    a. Wednesday afternoon

    b. After 8:00 a.m. on Wednesday

    c. At 8:00 a.m. on Wednesday

    d. Before 8:00 a.m. on Wednesday

2. The reason the message board is in a store in the middle of town is—

    a. the store was paid to put it there

    b. to make sure everyone sees it

    c. it is near Marlow Park

    d. it is near the Baptist Church

3. Who is the message board for?

    a. Only dog owners

    b. Everybody in the community

    c. Only people who are moving

    d. Everyone in the neighboring town

4. Which of these is a fact found on the message board?

    a. All of the dogs in the community have fleas.

    b. Mike needs his lawn mowed.

    c. Only the Baptist Church has a choir.

    d. The little league does not give players gloves.

5. Which of these does the Community Message Board most resemble?

    a. A story about another town

    b. A public notice about a Town Hall meeting

    c. A true story about the town

    d. A letter mailed to the Baptist Church

Oysterville Crate Race

Rita was excited when she noticed the poster in a store window. One of her favorite activities was the Oysterville Crate Race. She loved trying to keep her balance while she competed and everyone had so much fun when an unlucky contestant fell in the water. Rita was determined that this year she was going to be the winner!

Oysterville Crate Race

Who Can Enter?

Boys and girls who are:

Group 1: 50–100 pounds   Group 3: 150–200 pounds

Group 2: 100–150 pounds   Group 4: Above 200 pounds

When Is It?

August 15th

Rules for the Race

For the race, 50 wooden crates are tied together between two piers. The crates float on top of the water and racers try to balance themselves and run across the crates as fast as possible. If you make it across the crates, you must turn around and come back across the crates again. The object is to cross as many times as possible without falling off. One girl crossed over 2,300 crates. That means she crossed the 50 crates 46 times!

What You Need

You will need sneakers, a bathing suit, and good balance to race over as many crates as possible before you fall into the water.

Prizes

First place in each weight class wins $25. Runners-up in each weight class win oyster dinners.

Can you walk on water?

Well, maybe you can by stepping on a row of wooden crates. The Oysterville Crate Race is a crazy way to take a swim but a great way to have some fun.

There are many other races across crates in the water, but the Oysterville Crate Race was the world's first!

Oysterville Crate Race *(cont.)*

1. Why was Rita excited when she noticed the poster in a store window?

    a. She could wear her new bathing suit.

    b. The Oysterville Crate Race was one of her favorite activities.

    c. She had designed the poster.

    d. She won the race last year.

2. What is the object of the race?

    a. To win an oyster dinner

    b. To tie the crates between two piers

    c. To run back and forth on the crates as many times as possible

    d. To run across the crates the fastest

3. To improve her chance of winning, Rita could—

    a. read more posters

    b. practice running on the two piers

    c. practice running and keeping her balance

    d. practice swimming

4. What does the word contestant mean?

    a. Someone who watches a contest.

    b. Someone who invents a contest.

    c. Someone who enters a contest.

    d. Someone who judges a contest.

5. The purpose of the poster is to—

    a. let people know about the girl who ran across the crates 46 times.

    b. warn people that it is possible to fall off the crates.

    c. let people know that the Oysterville Crate Race is a great way to have fun.

    d. give people information about how to enter the race and what the race is all about.

Apricot Banana Shakes

Food You Will Need:

- 1 cup orange juice, chilled
- $\frac{1}{2}$ cup milk
- $\frac{1}{4}$ teaspoon vanilla
- 1 16-ounce can pitted apricot halves, chilled
- 1 banana
- ground nutmeg

Equipment You Will Need:

- measuring cups and spoons
- can opener
- blender
- drinking glasses

Directions:

1. Measure the orange juice, milk, and vanilla into the blender container. Add the apricots and their juice. Peel the banana. Break the banana into four pieces; add to the blender container.

2. With help from an adult, put the lid on the blender and blend the mixture until it is smooth. Pour the mixture into the glasses; sprinkle the top with a little nutmeg.

   Serve cold and enjoy

   Makes 4 servings

To make your table look special, add a vase of flowers and tie pretty ribbon bows around some colorful paper napkins. Use rusts, greens, and browns in the fall and pumpkins or gourds. A winter table looks nice with reds and greens and pinecones with ivy or greens from trees. Soft colors and small bunny decorations work well in the spring. Try any flower and color together during the summer. Red, white, and blue would make a perfect table for the 4th of July.

Apricot Banana Shakes *(cont.)*

1. When should you add the apricots?

    a. After you pour the mixture into the glasses

    b. After you set the table with a vase of flowers

    c. After you peel the banana and break it into four pieces

    d. After you measure the orange juice, milk, and vanilla into the blender

2. How much milk do you need?

    a. $\frac{1}{4}$ teaspoon

    b. 1 cup

    c. $\frac{1}{2}$ cup

    d. 16 ounces

3. To make an apricot banana shake, you do not need a—

    a. blender

    b. pumpkin

    c. can opener

    d. banana

4. Why did the author include the last paragraph?

    a. To show that apricot banana shakes should only be served on a table

    b. To show that the 4th of July is the best time to have a party

    c. To give ideas about how to decorate for the holidays

    d. To give ideas about how to serve apricot banana shakes

5. How can the reader better understand this recipe?

    a. Read the entire recipe before making the shake.

    b. Read a story about the inventor of apricot banana shakes.

    c. Read an article about the 4th of July.

    d. Read a story about a summer party.

Blowing Giant Bubbles!

Good friends, Hai and Dara, ride their bikes to the park. Today there is a gentle breeze blowing and this makes it a perfect day for making giant bubbles. At home, they had made a new bubble-blower using an old shirt. They had also created some giant-bubble-soap using a special recipe. Now Hai and Dara could make much bigger bubbles than were possible with the tiny bubble-wands stores sell. Dara had heard that the world-record bubble was over 100 feet long. She hoped that they could even make a bigger bubble. Making giant bubbles was going to be fun!

What You Need:

- scissors
- an old blanket
- sugar
- soap flakes or soap powder
- a large jar with a lid
- a painter's tray or other large, deep pan
- 4 cups of warm tap water
- measuring cups and spoons

Steps for making giant bubbles:

1. Use the scissors to cut a circular ring of cloth out of the old blanket. This ring will be your bubble "wand." A ring about three feet across is best.

2. Pour four cups of warm tap water into your jar.

3. Stir in four tablespoons of soap flakes (one tablespoon for each cup of water).

4. While the water is still warm, stir in four tablespoons of sugar.

5. Put the lid on the jar and let the bubble-soap sit for three days before using it.

Steps for making giant bubbles:

1. Take your giant bubble-blower and soap to an open area on a day when a light breeze is blowing.

2. Pour the bubble-soap into your painting tray or deep pan.

3. Dunk your cloth bubble-blower ring into the bubble-soap until it is soaked and pull the wet bubble-blower out of the tray or pan.

4. You and a friend can then gently pull the cloth-ring open. The bubble-soap will stay in a thin layer in the center of the ring.

5. Turn the circle into the breeze and watch the bubbles fly!

Blowing Giant Bubbles! *(cont.)*

1. In order to make giant bubbles, you need—

    a. a tin can

    b. sugar

    c. coffee

    d. paint

2. How much soap flakes are needed to make bubble soap?

    a. four cups

    b. four tablespoons

    c. one cup

    d. one tablespoon

3. One thing not important in the directions for making a giant bubble-blower is—

    a. the color of the old blanket

    b. letting the bubble-soap sit for three days before using it

    c. using soap flakes or soap powder

    d. cutting a circular ring out of the old blanket

4. Why did the author include the first paragraph?

    a. To say that Hai and Dara rode to the park to blow giant bubbles.

    b. To explain that Hai and Dara are good friends.

    c. To tell what supplies you need to make giant bubbles.

    d. To explain how to make the bubble mixture.

5. A good way to find the answer to the question just above this one is to—

    a. re-read the first paragraph and decide what the main idea of it is.

    b. skim the directions and look for clues.

    c. re-read the entire directions.

    d. look for the words "giant-bubble-soap" and then keep reading.

Gold-Star Adventure Books!

These adventure books by award-winning authors and illustrators present exciting and powerful stories.

Five Amazing Novels

- *Winter of the Wolf* by Amber Healey—When Lupita gets lost in the wilds of Wyoming, can she survive with the help of a special friend? Soft cover: 11-9048 ($4.95)

- *Dark Eyes* by Anita Marquez—Molly thought she was the only person in Laneville who knew about the old mill. But is she? Soft cover: 11-9049 ($4.95)

- *Old Champ* by Richard Balnikov—Marcos wanted a champion dog, not some old mutt. But after Champ saves his sister from drowning, Marcos begins to change his mind. Soft cover: 11-9050 ($3.95)

- *The Path of the Arrow* by Andrew Holliday—Set in the nineteenth century, this novel tells the story of two good friends from two different worlds. Can their friendship survive their differences? Soft cover: 11-9051 ($4.95)

- *People of the Trees* by Margaret DeMercier—Sterling knows something is going on in the woods behind her house. Is it possible that the trees are moving? You won't believe the ending to this strange and intriguing novel! Soft cover: 11-9052 ($5.95)

Save! Buy all five novels for only $19.95! Just use order number 11-9055.

To order, call 1-800-555-7725 or fax 1-800-555-7748.

A $.95 shipping and handling charge will be added for each item ordered; $4.75 if ordering all five books.

Gold-Star Book Catalogue, Winter

Gold-Star Books
A Division of HorizonBound Publishers, Inc.
P.O. Box 4713; Dept. 27Q
Willow Run, West Virginia 83442

Gold-Star Adventure Books! *(cont.)*

1. Lupita may need the help of a special friend. Who might that friend be?

   a. a bear

   b. a wolf

   c. a cougar

   d. a buffalo

2. *People of the Trees* is described as an intriguing novel. The novel will most likely be—

   a. interesting.

   b. boring.

   c. ordinary.

   d. amusing.

3. How are the books listed in the catalogue similar?

   a. They are all illustrated by the same person.

   b. They are all written by award-winning authors.

   c. They are all adventure stories about dogs.

   d. They are all priced the same.

4. *The Path of the Arrow* asks if the friendship of two people can survive their differences. Survive means—

   a. last in spite of.

   b. occur due to the lack of.

   c. happen because of.

   d. make fun of.

5. How much will shipping and handling be if all five books are ordered?

   a. $3.95

   b. $4.75

   c. $4.95

   d. $5.95

Windy Canyon Middle School

Bulletin for December 17

- Remember that Friday, December 21, is the last day of school before the holiday break. It is also teacher conference day, so the school will be in session only until 12:30 p.m.

- The fourth, fifth, and sixth graders will be presenting "Celebrations of the Season" on Wednesday, December 19 at 7:00 p.m. Admission to the show is free. Bring your whole family for some fun and lively holiday spirit!

- Mrs. Bowman had a baby girl on Sunday at 3:00 a.m. The baby weighs eight pounds, three ounces and is named Shakira June. Congratulations to the parents and their new daughter!

- Our librarian, Ms. Nelson, reminds everyone that reading a book is a great way to spend the holiday break. Come on in to the library. Ms. Nelson will be glad to recommend some of her favorite titles.

- Mr. Henderson will be presenting a science fair in March. Anyone who is interested in participating should see Mr. Henderson in room 23 to sign up.

- The Public Library Book Talkers are coming this week! Angie will be visiting rooms 24, 25, and 29 tomorrow. Mark will be visiting rooms 7, 10, and 12 on Thursday. Don't forget to bring your library cards! Only students with library cards will be allowed to check out books. Angie says she has some super-exciting choices this time, so be prepared!

- Tony D'Agostino lost a blue parka yesterday in the cafeteria. Has anyone found it? Please bring it to the office if you have. He is very cold without it.

- There are rumors that the Poetry Squad will be roving through classrooms today. Keep your eyes and ears open!

- Lunch today will be sloppy joes, french fries, green beans, and frosted brownies. Yum**!**

Our Windy Canyon Middle School Hunger Drive has collected over 2,500 cans of food so far! We want to express our many thanks to everyone who has participated. We will be dropping the cans off at the local homeless shelter Friday evening. Thist will help many families have a happier holiday season!

Windy Canyon Middle School *(cont.)*

1. Which of the following is in a form that could be posted in this bulletin?

    a. Reading, math, science, lunch, physical education, social studies

    b. After-School Enrichment classes begin on Thursday, January 17.

    c. The capital of the United States is Washington, D.C.

    d. The chairs in the cafeteria are orange and yellow plastic.

2. What would a Public Library Book Talker most likely say to a class?

    a. "Thank you for all the cans of food you have donated!"

    b. "Be sure to sign up for the March Science Fair."

    c. "If you like adventure stories, you'll love *Missing in the Mountains!*"

    d. "Remember the sing-along after 'Celebrations of the Season.'"

3. Why will Ms. Nelson recommend some good books?

    a. She wants the library empty so that she can clean it more easily.

    b. She wants students to be prepared so they can talk to Angie when she visits.

    c. She wants people to buy books so she can donate the money to the Hunger Drive.

    d. She wants students to do something both fun and educational over school vacation.

4. Why is there an announcement about Tony D'Agostino?

    a. He wants to find his lost coat because it is cold outside.

    b. He is selling frosted brownies for teacher conference day.

    c. His mother just had a baby, and he is proud of his new sister.

    d. He is helping Mr. Henderson organize the science fair.

5. Which of the following is an example of an opinion?

    a. Admission to the holiday show is free.

    b. The Public Library Book Talkers are coming this week!

    c. Mr. Henderson will be presenting a science fair in March.

    d. Angie has some super-exciting choices this time.

Directions: Read this story carefully. When you are completely finished answer the questions on the next page. Make sure to completely fill in the bubbles

Carrie's Musical Dream

For a long time Carrie had dreamed of being in the school band . Now her dream was finally coming true! She loved watching her older sister in parades and concerts. Carrie couldn't quite believe that she was going to be a part of that at last. Carrie knew that being in the school band took a lot of work and dedication, but she also knew that she could handle it.

Carrie had chosen the clarinet as her instrument, and her mother thought that it would be a good idea to get Carrie a few lessons before school started. That way Carrie could at least learn to read music and get started on the basics of clarinet playing. The high school offered music lessons for beginners, so Carrie's mom signed her up. Carrie was quite excited about this opportunity.

When the time came for her first lesson, Carrie made sure that her new clarinet was in its case and ready to go. She was nervous. She really wanted to do a good job and make her sister proud of her. Carrie's mother took her to the music building at the high school for the lesson. Mrs. Williams, the instructor, was waiting for them and greeted Carrie and her mother warmly. The adults chatted for a minute, and then Carrie's mom said that she would return in one hour. Carrie and Mrs. Williams went into the practice room next to the office and sat down behind a large, black music stand. Carrie's heart was pounding as she gently removed her clarinet from its case.

First, Mrs. Williams showed her how to put all the pieces together. Then, she went over all the basics, including how to hold the instrument and how to blow into the mouthpiece. Carrie listened intently to every word. When Mrs. Williams gave a nod, Carrie picked up her new clarinet and tried to play a few notes. A loud squeak issued forth from the instrument and Carrie was soon out of breath. Mrs. Williams said that was normal for beginners, but with practice, Carrie would get better. They continued to work together until the lesson was over, and Carrie agreed to practice every day. Carrie's mom arrived all too soon. Carrie thanked Mrs. Williams, and told her that she would see her next week. Carrie was very glad that she had started lessons, and was feeling much more confident about her chances of getting into the school band!

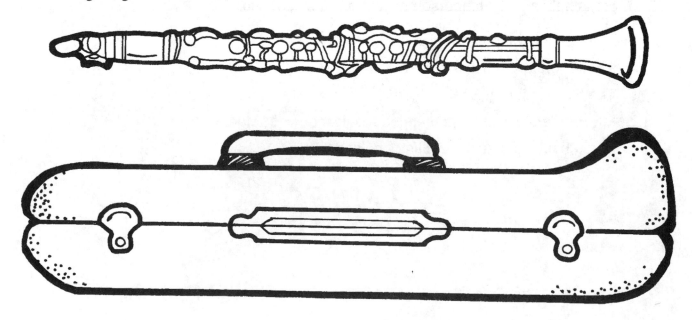

Carrie's Musical Dream *(cont.)*

1. Why did Carrie want to be in the school band?

   ⓐ Carrie's sister wanted Carrie to be in the band with her.

   ⓑ Carrie always liked to work hard.

   ⓒ Carrie wanted to be a part of the parades and concerts.

   ⓓ Carrie's mother wanted Carrie to learn to read music.

2. Why was the clarinet "in pieces"?

   ⓐ Carrie had not put it together yet.

   ⓑ Carrie had dropped the clarinet.

   ⓒ The clarinet was an old one that belonged to Carrie's mother.

   ⓓ Mrs. Williams wanted to show Carrie the parts of the clarinet.

3. What is the main idea of this story?

   ⓐ Music lessons are important.

   ⓑ Carrie is making her dream come true.

   ⓒ Carrie is a good student.

   ⓓ Everyone should have a dream.

4. What does it mean in the third paragraph when it states that Carrie's "heart was pounding"?

   ⓐ Carrie was out of breath from blowing so hard on her clarinet.

   ⓑ Carrie was excited to begin her music lesson.

   ⓒ Carrie was beginning to change her mind about taking lessons.

   ⓓ Carrie was upset that her mother had left.

5. How will Carrie's sister probably feel about Carrie being in the band?

   ⓐ She will be angry that Carrie is in the band, too.

   ⓑ Carrie's sister doesn't care about Carrie being in the band.

   ⓒ Carrie's sister will be excited to watch her older sister in the band.

   ⓓ Carrie's sister will be proud of Carrie.

Directions: Read this story carefully. When you are completely finished answer the questions on the next page. Make sure to completely fill in the bubbles

Clay

Clay has been used to make pottery and sculptures for hundreds of years. Early types of clay were dug from the earth. But not all earth can be used like clay. Clay is a special kind of earth that is good for making pottery. It holds together and dries completely. Baking clay in a very hot oven makes it hard. Once it has been baked, or "fired," clay becomes waterproof.

Ceramic artists today still use clay to make bowls and cups. But there are many other types of clay that artists can use. Several types of clay for hobby projects can be made from common things around the house. For example, clay can be made by mixing baking soda, cornstarch, and warm water. The mixture is cooked over low heat until it looks like oatmeal or mashed potatoes. After it has cooled, it can be handled like bread dough. This clay will be white, but it can be made any color by adding food coloring. It can also be painted after it has been shaped and dried.

One interesting form of modeling clay is actually made with lint from a clothes dryer! For this recipe, lint is put in a saucepan and covered with water. Then flour and a few drops of wintergreen mint flavoring are added. The ingredients are stirred together and cooked over low heat until the mixture becomes stiff. When it has cooled, this clay can be used to create small animal sculptures. It can even be shaped around a balloon and left to dry to make a clay ball!

Many kinds of hobby clay are sold in craft stores. Some are very colorful. Some dry as hard as a rock. Others, like Play-Doh®, shouldn't be allowed to dry.

The best thing about clay is that it has so many uses. With clay, artists can create many kinds of things. They can make tiny decorations. They can make huge statues for museums. They can even make pots and cups that will last many years. With clay, the possibilities are endless!

Clay *(cont.)*

1. What is probably the reason that artists like to use clay?
   (a) It can be made into many different things.
   (b) It can be dug from the earth.
   (c) It can be mixed with lint.
   (d) It can be sold in craft stores.

2. What does the author think about clay?
   (a) All clay should never be allowed to dry.
   (b) Clay has many uses.
   (c) Clay is not very useful.
   (d) Clay is good to eat.

3. According to the passage, how is clay made waterproof?
   (a) By mixing it with lint
   (b) By adding food coloring to it
   (c) By firing it
   (d) By kneading it like bread dough

4. What does the author mean when he states that the clay is "fired"?
   (a) The clay is baked.
   (b) The clay is washed.
   (c) The clay is formed.
   (d) The clay is painted.

5. Why would people probably want some of their clay objects to be waterproof?
   (a) Clay should never be waterproof.
   (b) Clay cannot be sold unless it is waterproof.
   (c) Clay cannot be used by artists unless it is waterproof.
   (d) Clay objects, such as bowls and cups, cannot be used unless they are waterproof.

Directions: Read this story carefully. When you are completely finished answer the questions on the next page. Make sure to completely fill in the bubbles

Sock Puppets

Puppets are fun to make and play with. This project is an easy way to make a hand puppet. Ask your parents for an old sock that you can use to make the puppet. If you can get a pair of socks, you can make two puppets and put on your own puppet shows!

What You Will Need:

- one or more socks (knee-high socks are best)
- felt-tip marker
- scissors
- buttons
- needle and thread
- felt
- yarn

What to Do:

1. Put the sock on your hand so that the toe area hangs down loosely from your fingers. Push the loose part into the palm of your hand, making a "mouth" for the puppet. (When you move your fingers and thumb, you can make the mouth move.)

2. Figure out where you want to place the eyes and nose on the puppet and mark each spot using the felt tip marker. (Be sure that the mark is clear enough to see when you take the sock off of your hand.)

3. Remove the sock from your hand and sew on buttons on the spots you marked for the eyes.

4. Cut a nose out of felt and sew it to the spot you marked for the nose. (You might want to cut out eyebrows and add them as well.)

5. Cut strings of yarn to use for hair. The length of the strings depends on how long you want your puppet's hair to be. Sew the strings of yarn onto the puppet.

6. Now you're ready to put the puppet on your hand and play with it. Think of what type of characters the puppet can be. Think of different ways you can make it act. Does your puppet have a funny voice? Can your puppet sing? How can you make your puppet dance? Get together with your friends and write some puppet plays to perform. You can even put puppets on both your hands and play two characters at the same time!

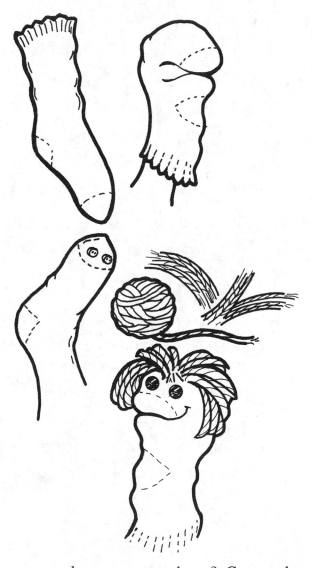

Sock Puppets *(cont.)*

1. This activity was probably taken from—
   - ⓐ a children's magazine.
   - ⓑ a dictionary.
   - ⓒ a world atlas.
   - ⓓ a textbook.

2. The instructions say "Figure out where you want to place the eyes and nose." Another way to say "figure out" is—
   - ⓐ draw a picture.
   - ⓑ put some glue.
   - ⓒ cut a hole.
   - ⓓ decide on.

3. For which steps do you need scissors?
   - ⓐ Steps 1 and 2
   - ⓑ Steps 1 and 3
   - ⓒ Steps 2 and 3
   - ⓓ Steps 4 and 5

4. What do you do with the felt-tip marker?
   - ⓐ Draw the eyes and nose on the puppet.
   - ⓑ Poke holes in the sock for the eyes and nose.
   - ⓒ Mark the spot for the eyes and nose.
   - ⓓ Measure the distance between the eyes and nose.

5. Which way of playing with the puppet does the writer not suggest?
   - ⓐ Making the puppet dance
   - ⓑ Making the puppet sing
   - ⓒ Making the puppet tell jokes
   - ⓓ Making the puppet talk in a funny voice

Practice Answer Sheet

This sheet may be reproduced and used with the reading comprehension questions. Each box can be used with one story. Using the answer sheets with the stories and questions gives extra practice in test preparation.

Page 5	Page 7	Page 9
1. (a) (b) (c) (d)	1. (a) (b) (c) (d)	1. (a) (b) (c) (d)
2. (a) (b) (c) (d)	2. (a) (b) (c) (d)	2. (a) (b) (c) (d)
3. (a) (b) (c) (d)	3. (a) (b) (c) (d)	3. (a) (b) (c) (d)
4. (a) (b) (c) (d)	4. (a) (b) (c) (d)	4. (a) (b) (c) (d)
5. (a) (b) (c) (d)	5. (a) (b) (c) (d)	5. (a) (b) (c) (d)

Page 11	Page 13	Page 15
1. (a) (b) (c) (d)	1. (a) (b) (c) (d)	1. (a) (b) (c) (d)
2. (a) (b) (c) (d)	2. (a) (b) (c) (d)	2. (a) (b) (c) (d)
3. (a) (b) (c) (d)	3. (a) (b) (c) (d)	3. (a) (b) (c) (d)
4. (a) (b) (c) (d)	4. (a) (b) (c) (d)	4. (a) (b) (c) (d)
5. (a) (b) (c) (d)	5. (a) (b) (c) (d)	5. (a) (b) (c) (d)

Page 17	Page 19	Page 21
1. (a) (b) (c) (d)	1. (a) (b) (c) (d)	1. (a) (b) (c) (d)
2. (a) (b) (c) (d)	2. (a) (b) (c) (d)	2. (a) (b) (c) (d)
3. (a) (b) (c) (d)	3. (a) (b) (c) (d)	3. (a) (b) (c) (d)
4. (a) (b) (c) (d)	4. (a) (b) (c) (d)	4. (a) (b) (c) (d)
5. (a) (b) (c) (d)	5. (a) (b) (c) (d)	5. (a) (b) (c) (d)

Practice Answer Sheet *(cont.)*

Page 23	Page 25	Page 27
1. (a) (b) (c) (d)	1. (a) (b) (c) (d)	1. (a) (b) (c) (d)
2. (a) (b) (c) (d)	2. (a) (b) (c) (d)	2. (a) (b) (c) (d)
3. (a) (b) (c) (d)	3. (a) (b) (c) (d)	3. (a) (b) (c) (d)
4. (a) (b) (c) (d)	4. (a) (b) (c) (d)	4. (a) (b) (c) (d)
5. (a) (b) (c) (d)	5. (a) (b) (c) (d)	5. (a) (b) (c) (d)

Page 29	Page 31	Page 33
1. (a) (b) (c) (d)	1. (a) (b) (c) (d)	1. (a) (b) (c) (d)
2. (a) (b) (c) (d)	2. (a) (b) (c) (d)	2. (a) (b) (c) (d)
3. (a) (b) (c) (d)	3. (a) (b) (c) (d)	3. (a) (b) (c) (d)
4. (a) (b) (c) (d)	4. (a) (b) (c) (d)	4. (a) (b) (c) (d)
5. (a) (b) (c) (d)	5. (a) (b) (c) (d)	5. (a) (b) (c) (d)

Page 35	Page 37	Page 39
1. (a) (b) (c) (d)	1. (A) (B) (C) (d)	1. (A) (B) (C) (d)
2. (a) (b) (c) (d)	2. (A) (B) (C) (d)	2. (A) (B) (C) (d)
3. (a) (b) (c) (d)	3. (A) (B) (C) (d)	3. (A) (B) (C) (d)
4. (a) (b) (c) (d)	4. (A) (B) (C) (d)	4. (A) (B) (C) (d)
5. (a) (b) (c) (d)	5. (A) (B) (C) (d)	5. (A) (B) (C) (d)

Answer Key

Flea Market Find, Page 5
1. b
2. b
3. b
4. b
5. c

Mona Wants A Dog, Page 7
1. a
2. d
3. d
4. c
5. b

My Cousin Douglas, Page 9
1. b
2. a
3. a
4. b
5. c

The Chess Champions, Page 11
1. d
2. a
3. d
4. b
5. b

Starting a Business, Page 13
1. b
2. d
3. a
4. d
5. a

New Faces, Page 15
1. c
2. b
3. d
4. b
5. b

Ladybugs, Page 17
1. d
2. c
3. b
4. a
5. d

Egyptian Pyramids, Page 19
1. d
2. d
3. a
4. b
5. c

Hot Dogs, Page 21
1. a
2. d
3. c
4. a
5. b

Galaxies, Page 23
1. b
2. c
3. b
4. c
5. c

How do You "Howdy Do"?, Page 25
1. a
2. a
3. d
4. a
5. b

Lighting the Way, Page 27
1. c
2. a
3. d
4. c
5. a

Community Message Board, Page 29
1. d
2. b
3. b
4. d
5. c

Oysterville Crate Race, Page 31
1. b
2. c
3. c
4. c
5. d

Apricot Banana Shakes, page 33
1. d
2. c
3. b
4. c
5. a

Blowing Giant Bubbles!, Page 35
1. b
2. b
3. a
4. a
5. a

Gold-Star Adventure Books!, Page 37
1. b
2. a
3. b
4. a
5. b

Windy Canyon Middle School, Page 39
1. c
2. c
3. d
4. a
5. d

Carrie's Musical Dream, Page 41
1. d
2. a
3. b
4. b
5. d

Clay, Page 43
1. a
2. b
3. c
4. a
5. d

Sock Puppets, Page 45
1. a
2. d
3. d
4. c
5. c